Letterland

Contents

Level 2 - Student Book 2

Story

This is Mr E's Magic **e**. The Silent Magic **e** shoots sparks over one letter to make a Vowel Man appear.

Silent Magic e!
You know this e you
cannot hear.
It can make a Vowel
Man appear.

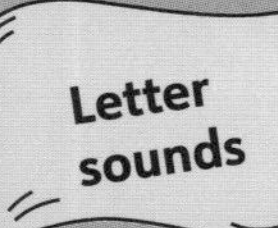

Look how the magic sparks shoot over one letter to make the Vowel Man appear and say his name.

Listen to the story about how Silent Magic e makes Mr U appear.

Magic e makes Mr U appear

Listen again to the story. This time look for the things in the picture in which Mr U has appeared to say his name.

Keywords

Find these items in the picture. Listen for Mr U saying his name in the words.

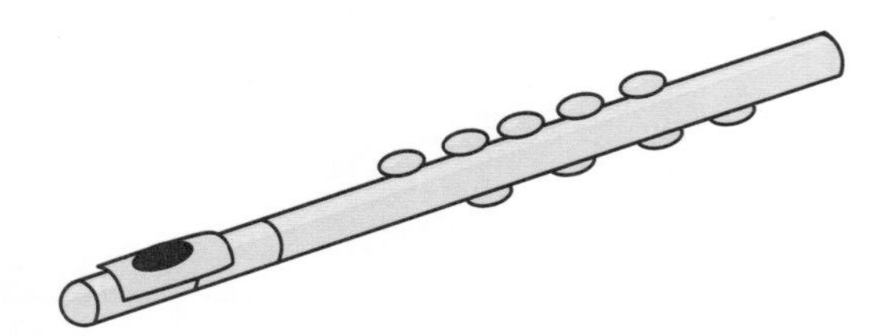

flute

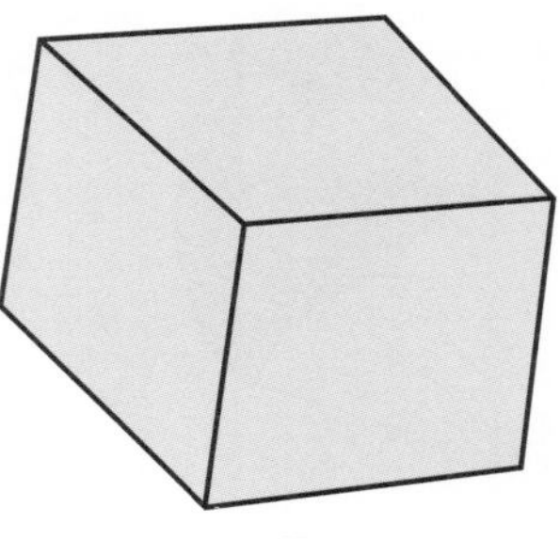

cube

parachute

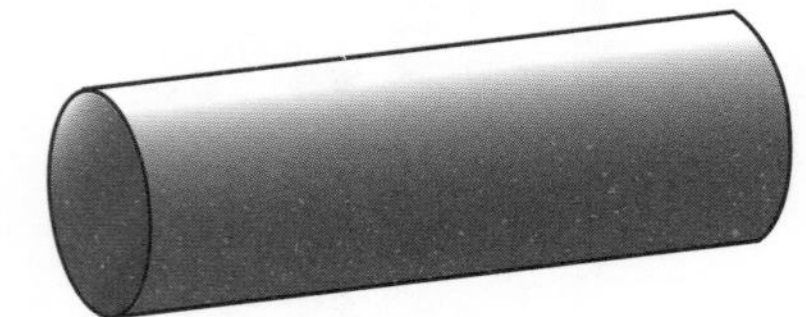

tube

perfume

Phonics Online

Listen to the story about Magic **e** making Mr U appear.
Sing along to the song, listen to the sound and play the games.

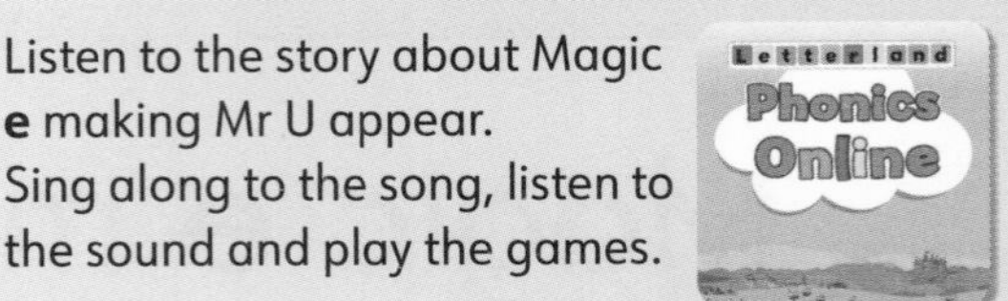

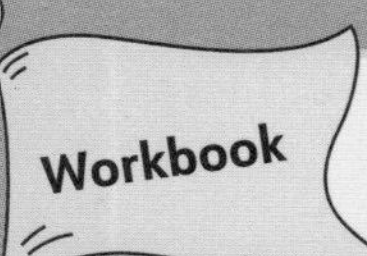

When you have finished this page, complete the **u_e** activities in *Workbook 2*, pages 2-4.

Note

Depending on accents, sometimes the **u_e** sound sounds a bit like **'oo'** but other times it sounds a bit like **'you'**.

(oo)

(you)

Build some **u_e** words using *Phonics Online*, or the *Picture Code Cards*.

Build it!

tube, cube

Let's read!

Read the sentence, then point to the correct picture.

He can play tunes on his flute.

Listen to the Magic **e** song. You should know this song now. Join in with the chorus when you listen for the second time.

Story

When Mr U and Mr E are out walking together, you'll hear Mr U saying his name. Listen to the reason why.

How do you do? I'm Mr U. You know I say, 'u'.

Greetings. I'm Mr E. I say my name, 'e'.

When we go out walking...

When these two vowels go out walking,
Mr U does the talking.

Mr U says his name, 'u', but his friend won't do the same.

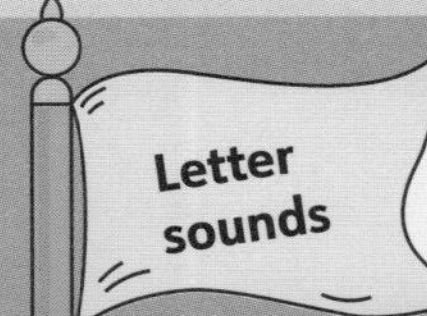

The first Vowel Man says his name. The second Vowel Man stays quiet. He's too busy looking out for robots.

Listen to the story about Mr U and Mr E out walking in words.

Mr U and Mr E out walking

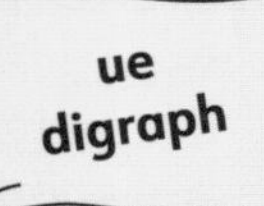

Listen again to the story. This time look for the things in the picture in which Mr U and Mr E are out walking in the word.

Keywords

Find these items in the picture. Listen for Mr U saying his name in the words.

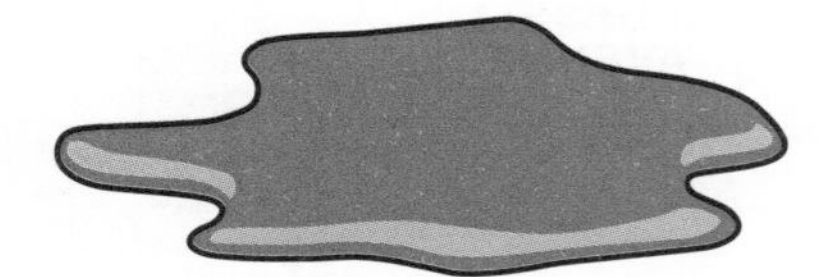

blue

glue

argue

Tuesday

barbecue

Phonics Online

Listen to the story about Mr U and Mr E out walking.
Sing along to the song, listen to the sound and play the games.

When you have finished this page, complete the **ue** activities in *Workbook 2*, pages 5-7.

Note

Sometimes the **ue** sound sounds a bit like '**oo**' but other times it sounds a bit like '**you**'.

(oo)

(you)

Build some **ue** words using *Phonics Online*, or the *Picture Code Cards*.

Build it!

blue, clue, glue, true.

Let's read!

Read the sentence, then point to the correct picture.

The glue is in a blue pot.

Listen to the Vowels Out Walking song. You should know this song now. Join in with the chorus when you listen for the second time.

Story

Let's meet these new friends.
Listen and try making the '**oo**' sound!

These are Mr O's grandsons. We call them the Boot and Foot Twins because they always argue over their boots.

When you hear an 'oo' sound in words, like boot, soon or zoo, it will be the Boot Twin saying...

"Oo! I have your boot!"

The Boot Twin says the sound you hear in boot. Sometimes you will hear the Foot Twin saying, 'Just look at my foot!' in words like book, cook and wood.

Explore Listen to the story about the Boot and Foot twins.

The Boot and Foot Twins

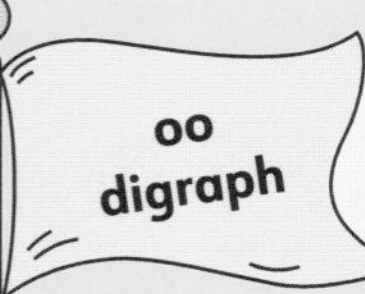

Listen again to the story. This time look for the things in the picture in which you can hear the Boot Twin saying **'oo'**.

Keywords

Find these items in the picture. Listen for the Boot twin saying '**oo**' in words.

zoo

boot

spoon

balloon

food

Phonics Online

Listen to the story about The Boot and Foot Twins.
Sing along to the song, listen to the sound and play the games.

When you have finished this page, complete the **oo** activities in *Workbook 2*, pages 8-10.

Word Building

Build some **oo** words using *Phonics Online*, or the *Picture Code Cards*.

Build it!

zoo, boot, spoon, food, moon.

Let's read!

Read the words, then point to the correct picture.

A kangaroo jumps in a pool.

He eats his food with a spoon.

Listen to the song. Try and join in with the '**oo**' sounds when you listen for the second time.

Story

Let's see what happens when Eddy Elephant and Walter Walrus meet in words.

I'm Eddy Elephant.
I say, 'e'.

I'm Walter Walrus.
I say, 'w'.

When we are together...

When these two sit together, Eddy quickly squirts water at Walter before he gets splashed himself! 'Oo, you!' Walter cries.

Letter sounds When you see these two letters together you will hear an **'oo'** or **'you'** sound (**'oo'** in chew; **'you'** in new).

Explore

Listen to the story about Eddy Elephant and Walter Walrus meeting in words.

Eddy Elephant and Walter Walrus

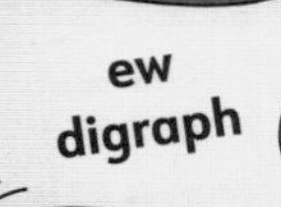

Listen again to the story. This time look for the things in the picture in which you can hear Walter saying '**ew**' or '**you**'!

Keywords

Find these items in the picture on the previous page. Listen for Walter saying **'oo'** or **'ew'** in the words.

news

jewels

cashews

stew

chew

Phonics Online

Listen to the story about Eddy Elephant and Walter Walrus. Sing along to the song, listen to the sound and play the games.

Workbook

When you have finished this page, complete the ew activities in *Workbook 2*, pages 11-13.

Word Building

Build some **ew** words using *Phonics Online*, the *Picture Code Cards* or Live Spelling.

Build it!

new, chew, threw,
jewel, cashew.

Let's read!

Use the Sound Slide trick to blend the sounds together and read the words. Then try reading the sentences with more fluency.

He has a
new hat.

She threw
the cashews.

Song

Listen to the song. Try and join in with the **'oo, you, oo, you**!' sounds at the end when you listen for the second time.

Track 114

Phonics Readers Read the stories in *Phonics Readers 6*, featuring the phonic elements in this Unit.

Comprehension

Point to the correct answer.

Stuck on a dune

Focus on: u_e, ue as in cube, blue

1. Who plays a tune on her flute?

○ Sue ☐ a cute cub

2. Who is cute?

○ the cub ☐ the tube

A day at the zoo

Focus on: oo as in moon

3. What did the zookeeper have on his feet?

○ black boots ☐ black buckets

4. Who rescued the baby penguin?

○ a kangaroo ☐ Aboo

The Hat Man's new roof

Tricky word: house

Focus on: ew, ew as in few, grew

5. What did Harry Hat Man eat for dinner?

○ a stew ☐ a new roof

Pair work When you have read the stories, the teacher will read the questions. Work in pairs or small groups to read and point to the correct answers.

Stickers Complete the sticker activity in *Workbook 2*, page 14.

Listen Complete the exercises in *Workbook 2*, pages 15-17.

Talk time

Learn the names of the musical instruments. Then work in pairs to talk about the characters playing instruments.

Who can you see in the picture?

Who is clapping to the tune?

violin

trumpet

recorder

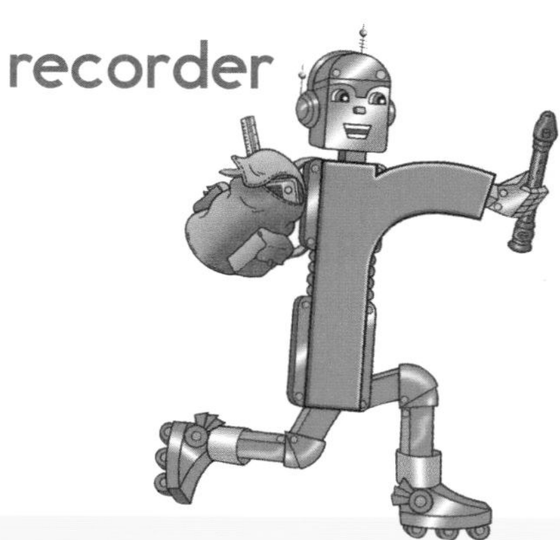

drum

flute

piano

What can he play?

He can play the flute.

Pair work In pairs, point to each picture and ask, 'What can he/she play?' Answer: 'He/She can play the...'. Then ask each other, 'What can you play?'.

Story

This is the robot gang. When you see a vowel behind a robot's back you will not hear its usual sound.

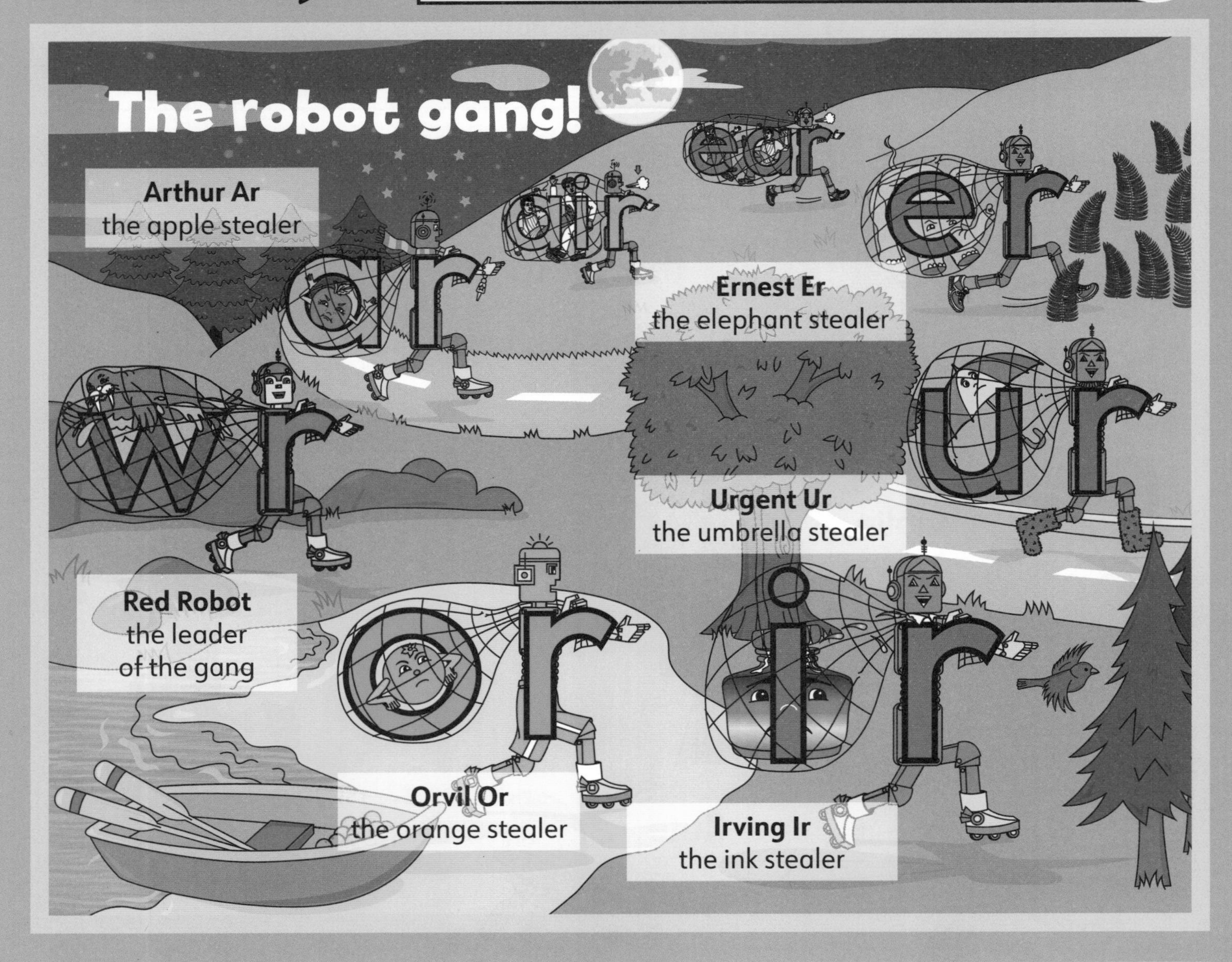

The Vowel Stealers!

Look out when there's a robot about! Don't expect the vowel behind his back to make the usual sound.

You will meet Arthur Ar and Orvil Or, then you will meet the three brothers who say **Er/Ir/Ur**.

Story

In the gang of vowel stealing robots, there is a robot called Arthur Ar. He steals apples.

Annie Apple usually says, 'a'

but...

Arthur Ar steals apples!

Arthur Ar steals apples.

As he runs off, he shouts, 'Ar!'

He runs away to his radar car.

Letter sounds Listen again to Arthur Ar saying his last name 'Ar' as he escapes in his radar car.

Listen to the story about Arthur Ar, the apple stealer.

Arthur Ar, the apple stealer

Listen again to the story. This time look for the things in the picture in which Arthur Ar is saying his name.

Keywords

Find these items in the picture. Listen for Arthur Ar stealing the apple and saying his name, **'Ar!'**.

stars

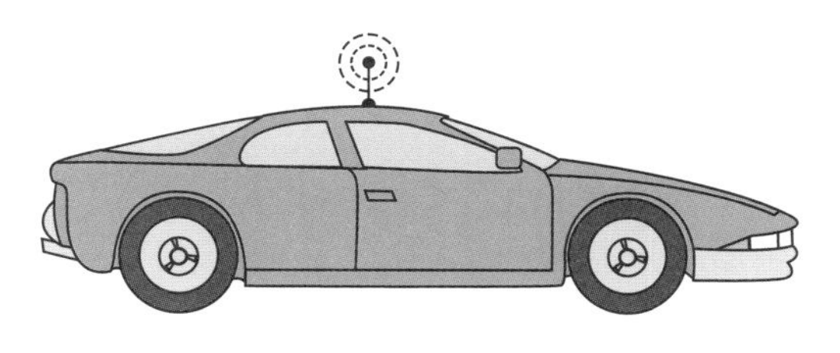

car

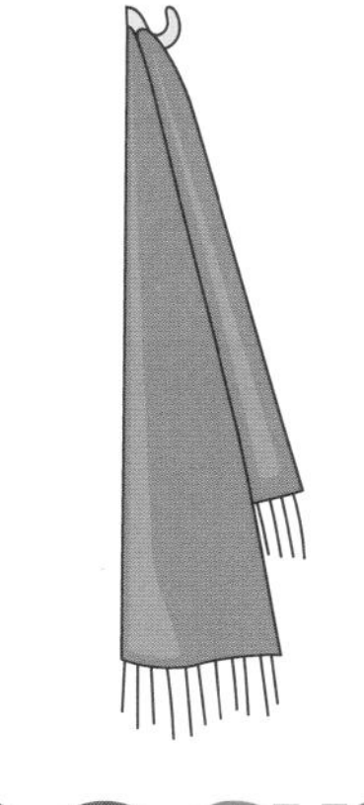

scarf

card

farmyard

Phonics Online

Listen to the story about Arthur Ar.
Sing along to the song, listen to the sound and play the games.

Workbook

When you have finished this page, complete the **ar** activities in *Workbook 2*, pages 18-20.

Word Building

Build some **ar** words using *Phonics Online*, or the *Picture Code Cards*.

Build it!

car, farm, scarf,
card, stars, hard.

Let's read!

Read the words, then point to the correct picture.

The car is in front of the farm.

We can see stars when it is dark.

Listen to Arthur Ar's song. If you can, join in with the chorus when you listen for the second time.

Story

In the gang of vowel stealing robots, there is a robot called Orvil Or. He steals oranges.

Oscar Orange usually says, 'o'

but...

Orvil Or steals oranges!

Orvil Or steals oranges.

As he runs off, he shouts, 'Or!'

He runs away to his boat by the shore.

Letter sounds When you see these two letters together you will hear Orvil Or shouting his last name, 'or!'.

Explore Listen to the story about Orvil Or, the orange stealer.

Orvil Or, the orange stealer

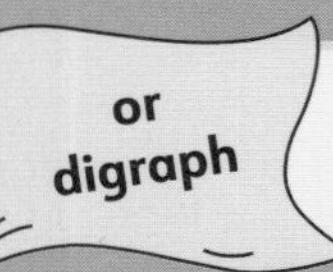

Listen again to the story. This time look for the things in the picture in which Orvil Or has appeared to say his name.

Keywords

Find these items in the picture. Listen for Orvil Or saying his last name in the words.

storm

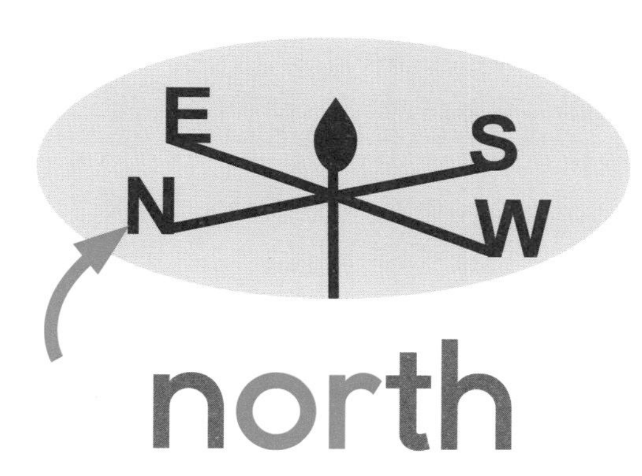

north

sport

Phonics Online

Listen to the story about Orvil Or.
Sing along to the song, listen to the sound and play the games.

Workbook

When you have finished this page, complete the **or** activities in *Workbook 2*, pages 21-23.

Workbook

Word Building

Build some **or** words using *Phonics Online*, or the *Picture Code Cards*.

Build it!

for, storm,

north, sport.

Let's read!

Use the Sound Slide trick to blend the sounds together and read the words. Then try reading the sentences with more fluency.

The storm is
in the north.

We like to play
lots of sport.

Listen to Orvil Or's song. If you can, join in with the chorus when you listen for the second time.

Story

In the gang of vowel stealing robots, there are three brothers. They all make the same sound but steal different vowels.

Optional: Listen to the three brothers song.

We are the Robot Brothers. If you see any vowels behind our backs, don't expect to hear the usual vowel sounds!

Ernest Er steals elephants!

Ernest Er steals elephants.

As he runs off, he shouts, 'Er!'
He is a faster runner than his other brothers.

Letter sounds When you see these two letters together you will hear Ernest Er shouting his last name, 'er!'.

Explore Listen to the story about Ernest Er, the elephant stealer.

Ernest Er, the elephant stealer

er digraph

Listen again to the story. This time look for the things in the picture in which Ernest Er is shouting out his name.

Keywords

Find these items in the picture. Listen for Ernest Er.
Can you think of any more words that end in 'er'?

tiger

danger

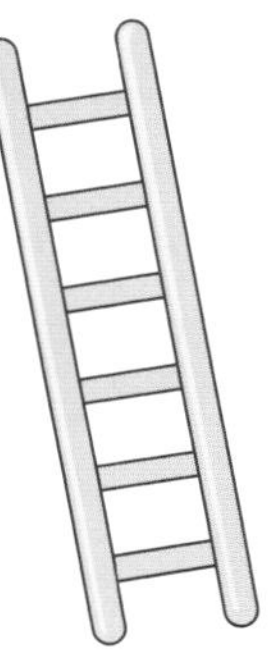

ladder

hammer

painter

Phonics Online

Listen to the story about Ernest Er.
Sing along to the song, listen to the sound and play the games.

Workbook When you have finished this page, complete the **er** activities in *Workbook 2*, pages 24-26.

Word Building

Build some **er** words using *Phonics Online*, or the *Picture Code Cards*.

Build it!

farmer, teacher, painter, runner, flower.

Let's read!

Use the Sound Slide trick to blend the sounds together and read the words. Then try reading the sentences with more fluency.

The insects like the flowers.

The painter went up the ladder.

Listen to Ernest Er's song. If you can, join in with the chorus when you listen for the second time.

Story

In the gang of vowel stealing robots, there are three brothers. They all make the same sound but steal different vowels.

We are the Robot Brothers. If you see any vowels behind our backs, don't expect to hear the usual vowel sounds!

Irving Ir steals ink!

Irving Ir steals ink.

As he runs off, he shouts, 'Ir!'

Letter sounds

When you see these two letters together you will hear Irving Ir shouting his last name, 'ir!'.

Explore Listen to the story about Irving Ir, the ink stealer.

Irving Ir, the ink stealer

Can you find thirteen birds in the big picture?

ir digraph Listen again to the story. This time look for the things in the picture in which Irving Ir is shouting out his name.

Keywords

Find these items in the picture. Listen for Irving Ir saying his name in the words.

bird

shirt

When is your birthday?

birthday

skirt

girl

Phonics Online

Listen to the story about Irving Ir.
Sing along to the song, listen to the sound and play the games.

Workbook

When you have finished this page, complete the ir activities in *Workbook 2*, pages 27-29.

Word Building

Build some **ir** words using *Phonics Online*, or the *Picture Code Cards*.

Build it!

skirt, shirt,
bird, girl, dirt.

Let's read!

Use the Sound Slide trick to blend the sounds together and read the words. Then try reading the sentences with more fluency.

This girl has got a dirty skirt.

This girl has got a clean skirt.

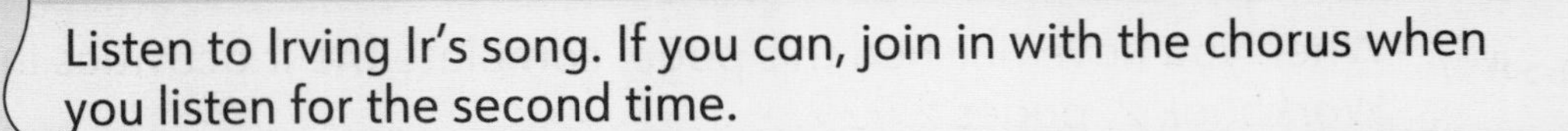

Listen to Irving Ir's song. If you can, join in with the chorus when you listen for the second time.

Story

In the gang of vowel stealing robots, there are three brothers. They all make the same sound but steal different vowels.

We are the Robot Brothers. If you see any vowels behind our backs, don't expect to hear the usual vowel sounds!

Urgent Ur steals umbrellas!

Urgent Ur steals umbrellas.

As he runs off, he shouts, 'Ur!'

Letter sounds

When you see these two letters together you will hear Urgent Ur shouting his last name, 'ur!'.

Explore Listen to the story about Urgent Ur, the umbrella stealer.

Urgent Ur, the umbrella stealer

ur digraph

Listen again to the story. This time look for the things in the picture in which Urgent Ur is shouting out his name.

Keywords

Find these items in the picture. Listen for Urgent Ur saying his name in these words.

nurse

purse

burger

fur

purple

Phonics Online

Listen to the story about Urgent Ur.
Sing along to the song, listen to the sound and play the games.

Workbook

When you have finished this page, complete the **ur** activities in *Workbook 2*, pages 30-32.

Word Building

Build some **ur** words using *Phonics Online*, or the *Picture Code Cards*.

Build it!

fur, turn, curl,

burger, Thursday.

Let's read!

Use the Sound Slide trick to blend the sounds together and read the words. Then try reading the sentences with more fluency.

She sells burgers
on Thursday.

He has fur boots.

Song

Listen to Urgent Ur's song. If you can, join in with the chorus when you listen for the second time.

Track 140

Story

Red Robot knows that Walter Walrus is a troublemaker so he quickly grabs Walter in his sack. Walter Walrus is too startled to speak.

Walter Walrus usually says, 'w'

but...

Red Robot captures Walter Walrus!

Red Robot captures Walter Walrus.

As he runs off he shouts, 'r!'

Letter sounds

When you see these two letters together you will just hear Red Robot as Walter Walrus is too startled to speak.

Explore Listen to the story about Red Robot running off with Walter Walrus.

Red Robot captures Walter Walrus

wr digraph

Listen again to the story. This time look for the things in the picture in which Red Robot is growling his name.

Keywords

Find these items in the picture. Listen for Red Robot growling his name in these words.

write

wriggle

wreck

wrapper

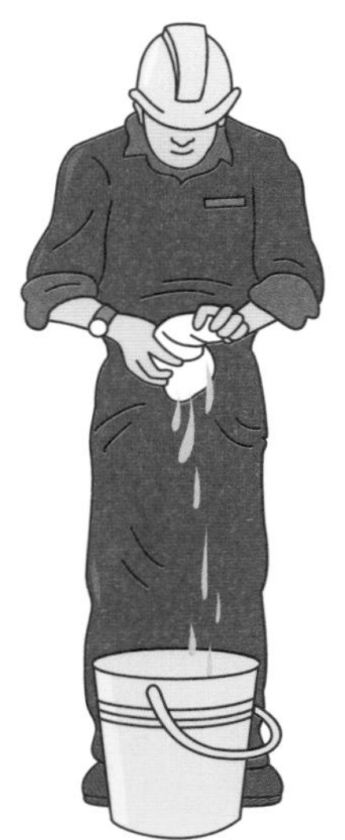

wring

Phonics Online

Listen to the story about Walter Walrus and Red Robot.
Sing along to the song, listen to the sound and play the games.

Workbook

When you have finished this page, complete the wr activities in *Workbook 2*, pages 33-35.

Word Building

Build some **wr** words using *Phonics Online*, or the *Picture Code Cards*.

Build it!

write, wreck,

wring, wrapper.

Let's read!

Use the Sound Slide trick to blend the sounds together and read the words. Then try reading the sentences with more fluency.

She writes lots of letters.

This is a wreck.

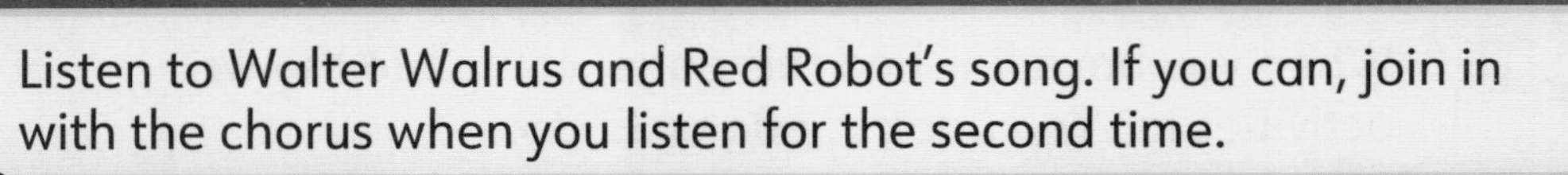

Listen to Walter Walrus and Red Robot's song. If you can, join in with the chorus when you listen for the second time.

Phonics Readers Read the stories in *Phonics Readers 7*, featuring the phonic elements in this Unit.

Comprehension

Point to the correct answer.

1. What did Nick get from the store?

○ sweetcorn ☐ sweet cakes

2. What can Peter do well?

○ sing ☐ read

3. What did Swirly Bird want to wear?

○ a red skirt ☐ a pink skirt

4. What is the name of the dog in this story?

○ Furry ☐ Curly

Pair work When you have read the stories, the teacher will read the questions. Work in pairs or small groups to read and point to the correct answers.

Stickers Complete the sticker activity in *Workbook 2*, pages 36.

Listen Complete the exercises in *Workbook 2*, pages 37-39.

Talk time Let's learn about countries/regions and how to say where we are from. Listen first. Then you try. Change partners and repeat.

Where are you from?

Angola
Belgium
Canada
Denmark
Ecuador
Fiji
Greece
Hong Kong
India
Japan
Korea
Libya
Malaysia
Nigeria
Oman
Pakistan
Qatar
Russia
Singapore
Taiwan
UK
Vietnam
Yemen
Zimbabwe

Above are just a few countries /regions in alphabetical order. Challenge: get out an atlas and find as many countries/regions as you can starting with a chosen letter.

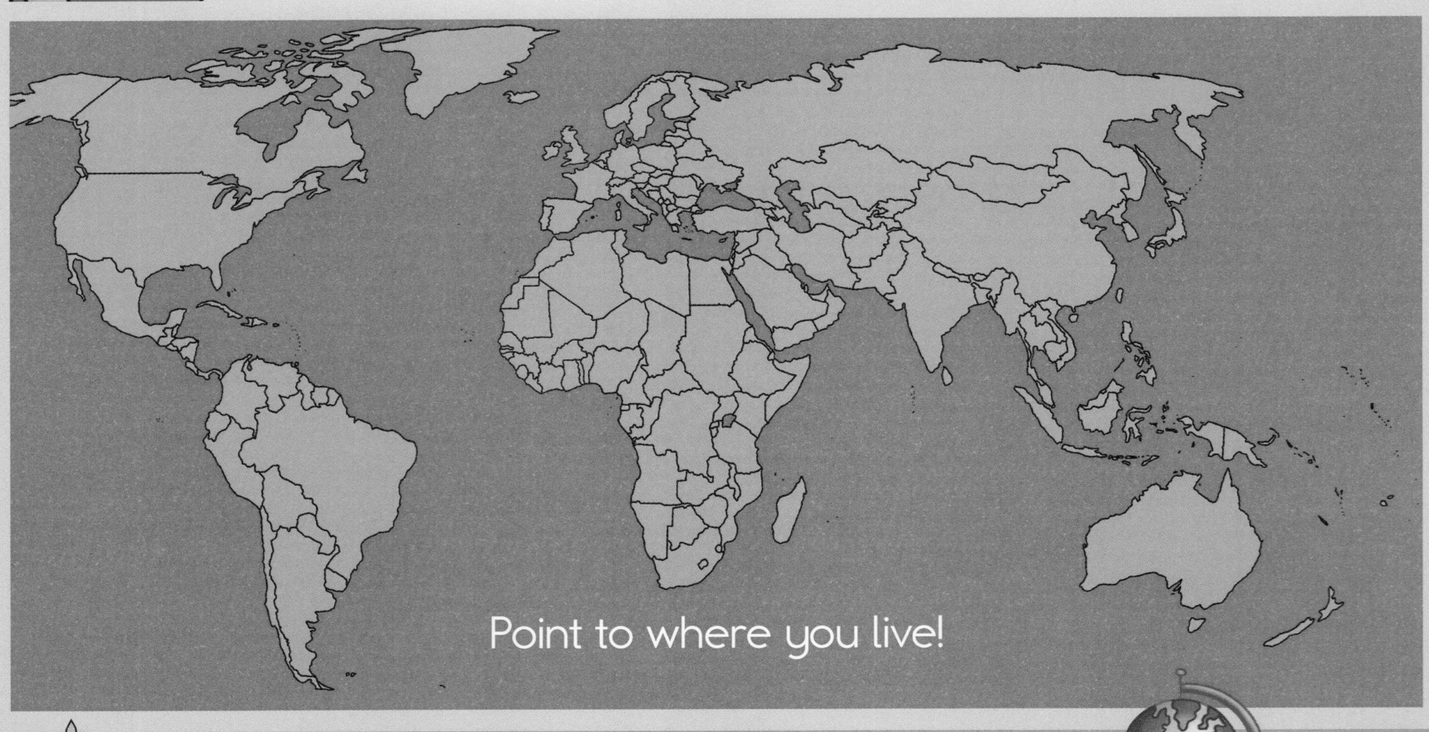

The world Point to where you live on the map.

Story

Oscar Orange has a Little Brother, but he has not learned how to say Oscar's sound. Listen to what happens.

Oscar Orange has a little brother.

Oscar's Bothersome Little Brother

Oscar's Bothersome Little Brother can't say 'o' like Oscar. Instead he just says, 'uh'.

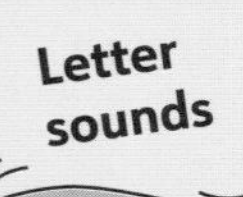

Letter sounds

Use your *Picture Code Cards* to review Oscar Orange and the new sound of Oscar's Bothersome Little Brother.

Listen to the story about Oscar's Bothersome Little Brother.

Oscar's Bothersome Little Brother

Listen again to the story. This time look for the things in the picture in which you can hear Oscar's Bothersome Little Brother saying '**o**'.

Keywords

Find these items in the picture. Listen for Oscar's Bothersome Little Brother's '**o**' sound in them.

monkey

money

son

dove

honey

Phonics Online

Listen to the story about Oscar's Bothersome Little Brother. Sing along to the song, listen to the sound and play the games.

When you have finished this page, complete the o activities in *Workbook 2*, pages 40-42.

Word Building

Build some **o** words using *Phonics Online*, or the *Picture Code Cards*.

Code Card

Build it!

son, won, brother, mother.

Let's read!

Use the Sound Slide trick to blend the sounds together and read the words. Then try reading the sentences with more fluency.

This mother has a son.

She won the race!

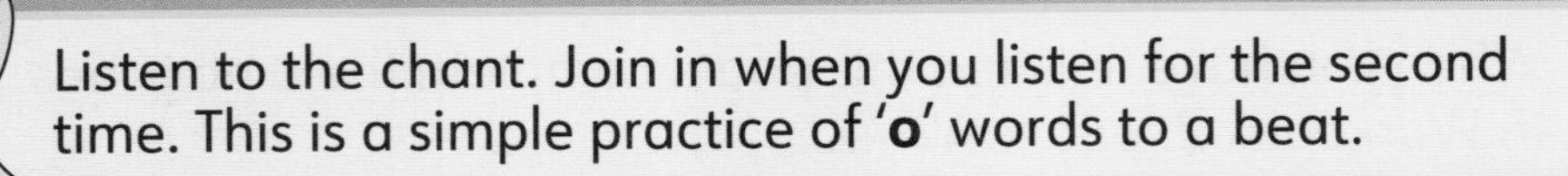

Listen to the chant. Join in when you listen for the second time. This is a simple practice of '**o**' words to a beat.

Story

Look! It's the Boot and Foot Twins.
Listen and try making the Foot Twin's '**oo**' sound!

Look! It's the Boot and Foot Twins again! They always argue over their boots. You have already met the Boot Twin.

When you say words like foot, look or book, you will be hearing the Foot Twin's sound. Here he is saying 'oo' again.

Instead of hearing the Boot Twin's sound, you will hear the Foot Twin's sound in these words: b**oo**k, c**oo**k and w**oo**d.

Listen to the story about The Boot and Foot Twins.

The Boot and Foot Twins

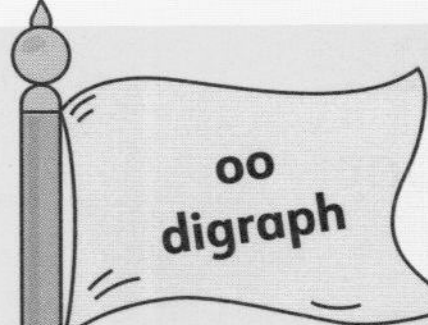

Listen again to the story. This time look for the things in the picture in which you can hear the Foot Twin saying **'oo'**.

Keywords

Find these items in the picture. Listen for the Foot Twin's '**oo**' sound in them.

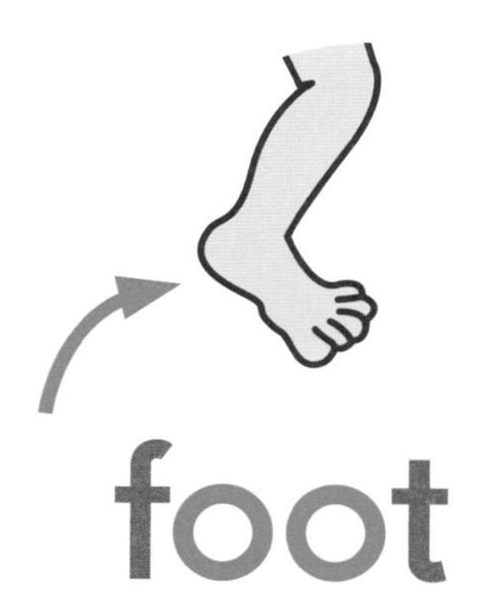

foot

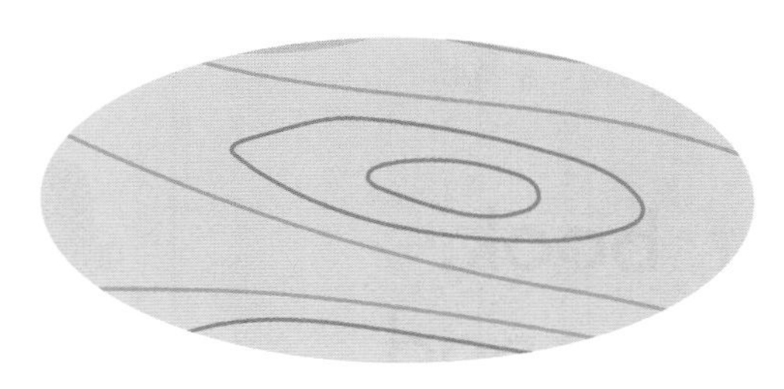

wood

book

hood

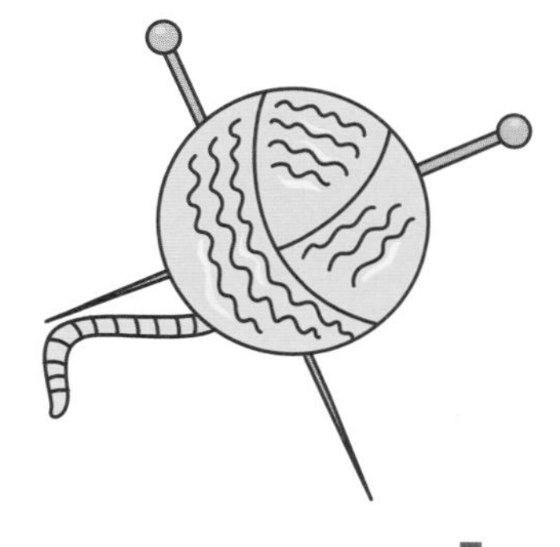

wool

Phonics Online

Listen to the story about The Boot and Foot Twins.
Sing along to the song, listen to the sound and play the games.

When you have finished this page, complete the **oo** activities in *Workbook 2*, pages 43-45.

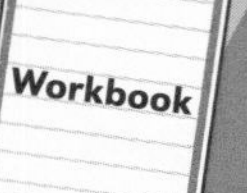

Word Building

Build some **oo** words using *Phonics Online*, or the *Picture Code Cards*.

Code Card

Build it!

foot, book, wood, good, hood.

Let's read!

Read the words, then point to the correct picture.

Look! Lots of good books!

She put up her hood in the rain.

Listen to The Boot and Foot Twins's song. If you can, join in with the chorus when you listen for the second time.

Story

Giant Full helps Mr U put umbrellas in words, but sometimes he can be rough. Listen to what happens.

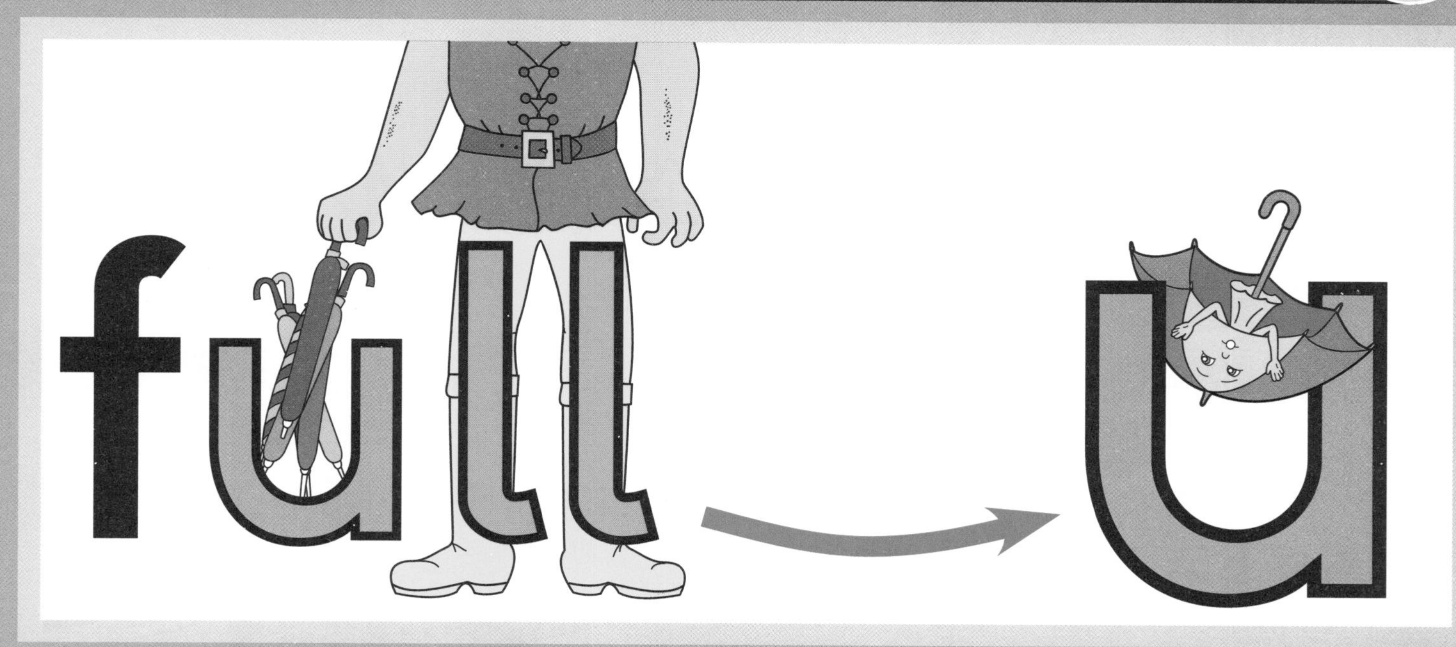

Upside Down Umbrella!

When umbrellas get pushed into their letter shapes upside down, they don't make the usual sound.

Letter sounds Use your *Picture Code Cards* to review Uppy Umbrella and the new sound of the Upside Down Umbrella.

Listen to the story about Uppy Umbrella being pushed upside down.

Upside Down Umbrella

Listen again to the story. This time look for the things in the picture in which you can hear an Upside Down Umbrella.

Keywords

Find these items in the picture. Listen for the Upside Down Umbrella.

push

pull

bull

full

bush

Phonics Online

Listen to the story about Upside Down Umbrella.
Sing along to the song, listen to the sound and play the games.

Workbook

When you have finished this page, complete the **u** activities in *Workbook 2*, pages 46-48.

Word Building

Build some **u** words using *Phonics Online*, or the *Picture Code Cards*.

Build it!

push, bush,
pull, bull, full.

Let's read!

Use the Sound Slide trick to blend the sounds together and read the words. Then try reading the sentences with more fluency.

The cup is full.

He pushed and pulled the bull.

Listen to the chant. Join in when you listen for the second time. This is a simple practice of **'u'** words to a beat.

Story

Let's meet a boy in Letterland called Roy.

Let's play the 'oy game'!

There's a boy called Roy in Letterland. Roy enjoys leaping over an 'o' into the Yo-yo Man's sack. Roy shouts 'oy' as he leaps. Yo-yo Man shouts 'oy' as he pretends to be annoyed!

Listen and leap up or clap if you hear the **'oy'** sound in the word.

Listen and leap!

toy	hot	employ
boy	enjoy	sort
hello	about	destroy

You will normally see Roy leaping over an **'o'** into Yellow Yo-yo Man's sack at the **end** of words.

Listen to the story about Roy leaping over an 'o' in a toy shop and landing in Yellow Yo-yo Man's sack.

Roy and Yellow Yo-yo Man

Listen again to the story. This time look for the things in the picture in which you can hear Roy and Yellow Yo-yo Man saying '**oy**'.

Keywords

Find these items in the picture. Listen for Roy playing the 'oy game' in these words.

toys

boy

destroy

annoyed

soy

Phonics Online

Listen to the story about Roy and Yellow Yo-yo Man.
Sing along to the song, listen to the sound and play the games.

When you have finished this page, complete the **oy** activities in *Workbook 2*, pages 49-51.

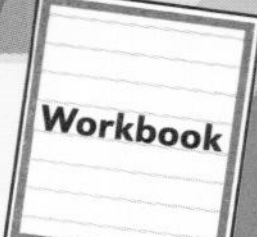

Word Building

Build some **oy** words using *Phonics Online*, or the *Picture Code Cards*.

Code Card

Build it!

toy, boy, soy,
annoy.

Let's read!

Use the Sound Slide trick to blend the sounds together and read the words. Then try reading the sentences with more fluency.

This room is
a mess! Pick up
the toys.

The boys like to
play with toys.

Listen to Roy and Yellow Yo-yo Man's song. If you can, join in when you listen for the second time.

Track 164

Story

What is this boy Roy doing now? He's playing the 'oi game' with Mr I.

Let's play the 'oi game'!

From time to time Mr I likes to join Roy in the game but only when they can play inside words. Remember Mr I gets dizzy at the end of words.

Listen and leap up if you hear the '**oi**' sound in the word.

Listen and leap!

hot	noise	toilet
coin	join	sort
nose	toe	

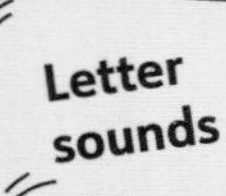

You will normally see Roy leaping over an 'o' onto Mr I's back in the **middle** of words.

Listen to the story about Roy leaping over an 'o' onto Mr I.

Roy and Mr I play the 'oi game'

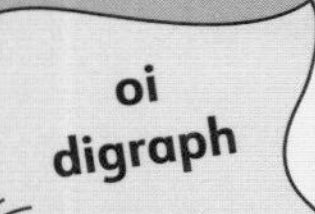

Listen again to the story. This time look for the things in the picture in which Roy and Mr I are saying '**oi**'.

Keywords

Find these items in the picture. Listen for Roy and Mr I playing the 'oi game' in these words.

boil

oil

soil

coins

noise

Phonics Online

Listen to the story about Roy and Mr I.
Sing along to the song, listen to the sound and play the games.

Workbook

When you have finished this page, complete the **oi** activities in *Workbook 2*, pages 52-54.

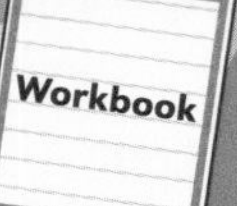

Word Building

Build some **oi** words using *Phonics Online*, or the *Picture Code Cards*.

Build it!

boil, soil,
oil, coin,
toilet.

Let's read!

Use the Sound Slide trick to blend the sounds together and read the words. Then try reading the sentences with more fluency.

Look! A coin in the soil!

This pan is full of hot oil.

Listen to Roy and Mr I's song. If you can, join in when you listen for the second time.

Phonics Readers Read the stories in *Phonics Readers 8*, featuring the phonic elements in this Unit.

Comprehension

Point to the correct answer.

1. Which item of clothing did Oscar Orange drop on the path?

◯ boots ☐ gloves

2. What did Clever Cat put on to go into the garden?

◯ gloves ☐ a wool cape

Nick's noisy new toy

Focus on: oy, oi as in boy, coin

3. What can Noisy Nick's robot pick up?

◯ toys ☐ coins

4. Who does Nick go to play with?

◯ Rob ☐ Roy

Pair work When you have read the stories, the teacher will read the questions. Work in pairs or small groups to read and point to the correct answers.

Stickers

Complete the sticker activity in *Workbook 2*, pages 55.

Listen

Complete the exercises in *Workbook 2*, pages 56-57.

Talk time

First look at the toys and say what they are. Then work in pairs to compare the toys with the questions below.

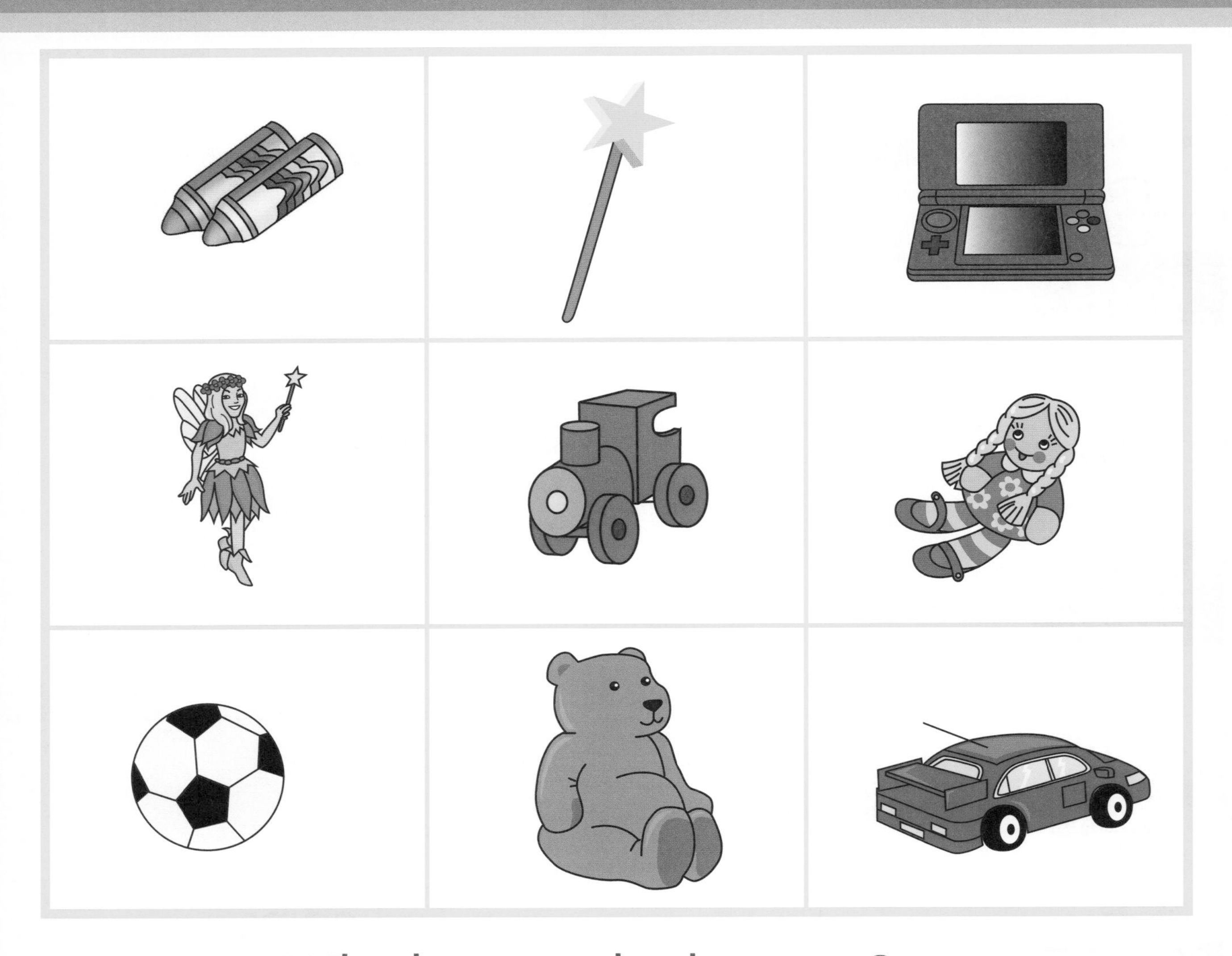

1. Which toy is the biggest?
2. Which toy is the smallest?
3. Which toy is the noisiest?
4. Which toy is the softest?
5. Which toy is the fastest?

Pair work

Work in pairs to ask and answer the questions.
Can you think of any more ways to compare these toys?

Story

Let's see what happens when Walter Walrus sits next to Annie Apple in a word.

Walter Walrus's water tricks!

Remember, when you see Walter Walrus in a word, expect trouble! Walter likes to splash water.

2 letters: 1 sound

When you see these two letters together, you will just hear Annie Apple shouting, '**Aw**! Don't be so **aw**ful!'

When you see Walter next to Annie Apple in a word, you won't hear Annie making her usual sound. Why not? Because Walter splashes her with salty water.

She cries out,

'Aw! Don't be so awful!'

Letter sounds

Use your *Picture Code Cards* to review the sound Annie Apple makes when next to Walter Walrus.

Listen to the story about Walter Walrus splashing Annie Apple with salty water.

Walter Walrus and Annie Apple

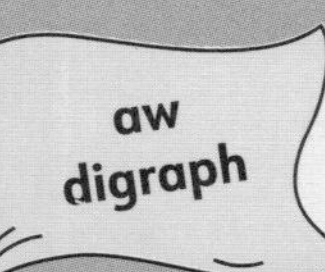

Listen again to the story. This time look for the things in the picture in which you can hear Annie saying, '**aw**!'

Keywords

Find these items in the picture. Listen for Annie saying '**aw**!' in these words.

jigsaw

yawn

straw

paw

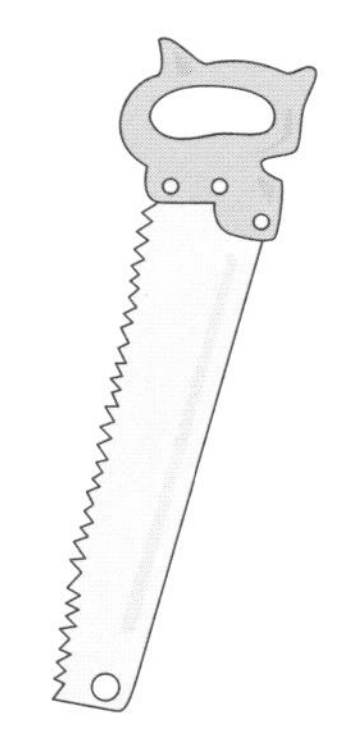

saw

Phonics Online

Listen to the story about Annie Apple and Walter Walrus. Sing along to the song, listen to the sound and play the games.

Workbook

When you have finished this page, complete the **aw** activities in *Workbook 2*, pages 58-60.

Word Building

Build some **aw** words using *Phonics Online*, or the *Picture Code Cards*.

Build it!

saw, paw, yawn,
lawn, straw, awful.

Let's read!

Read the sentence, then point to the correct picture.

He did not use a straw to drink his strawberry milk.

Listen to the chant. Join in when you listen for the second time.
This is a simple practice of '**aw**' words to a beat.

Story

Let's see what happens when Walter Walrus hides in Uppy's letter next to Annie Apple in a word.

Walter Walrus's water tricks!

Remember, when you see Walter Walrus in a word, expect trouble! Walter likes to splash water.

2 letters: 1 sound

When you see these two letters together, you will just hear Annie Apple shouting, '**Au**! Don't be n**au**ghty!'

Sometimes Walter is so naughty he fills Uppy Umbrella's letter with water and jumps in. He can then splash Annie Apple with salty water again.

She cries out, 'Au!

Don't be naughty!'

Letter sounds

Use your *Picture Code Cards* to review the sound.

Code Card

Listen to the story about Walter naughtily hiding in Uppy's letter.

Annie Apple & Walter in Uppy's letter

Listen again to the story. This time look for the things in the picture in which you can hear Annie saying, '**au**!'

Keywords

Find these items in the picture. Listen for Annie saying '**au**!' in them.

autumn

astronaut

saucer

launch

caution

Phonics Online

Listen to the story about Annie Apple and Walter in Uppy's letter. Sing along to the song, listen to the sound and play the games.

Workbook

When you have finished this page, complete the **au** activities in *Workbook 2*, pages 61-63.

Word Building

Build some **au** words using *Phonics Online*, or the *Picture Code Cards*.

Build it!

launch, haunt, sauce, saucer.

Chant

Listen and join in with the Annie Apple and Walter Walrus chant.

Read

Read the story once on your own. Then read it again out loud to your partner. Then listen and follow as your partner reads it to you.

On a cold day in ,  went to see a rocket

launch. She had to wait a long time for the launch so she did a . She waited again, then started to .

Soon, she fell asleep. She did not see the  get

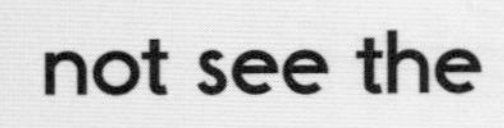

into the rocket. She did not see the rocket launch. She opened her eyes but she just saw the 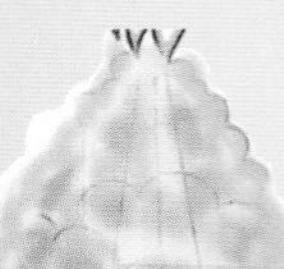! "Aw! How awful!"

Autumn jigsaw astronaut Annie Apple yawn exhaust

Stickers

Complete the sticker activity in *Workbook 2*, page 64.

Listen

Complete the exercises in *Workbook 2*, pages 66-67.

Story

Let's see what happens when Walter Walrus sits next to Oscar Orange in a word.

Walter Walrus's water tricks!

Watch out when Walter Walrus is about!

Do you remember the story about Mr O protecting Oscar? Mr O helps out whenever he's around, but when Mr O is away, Walter starts his water tricks again!

Sometimes when you see Oscar and Walter together you will hear a very different sound. This is because Walter tries to splash Oscar again. But as Walter splashes, he slips and bumps his chin. Now, they both howl, 'Ow!'

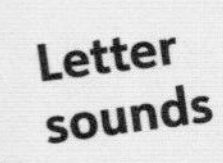

Letter sounds

Use your *Picture Code Cards* to review the sound. Look at the two sounds of '**ow**'.

Listen to the story about Walter Walrus splashing Oscar Orange with salty water.

Oscar Orange and Walter Walrus

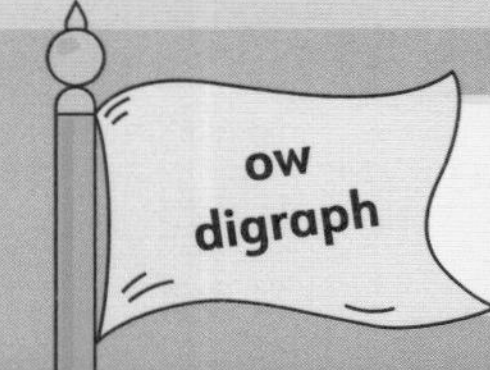

Listen again to the story. This time look for the things in the picture in which you can hear Oscar and Walter howling, '**ow**!'

Keywords

Find these items in the picture. Listen for Oscar and Walter howling, '**ow**!' in these words.

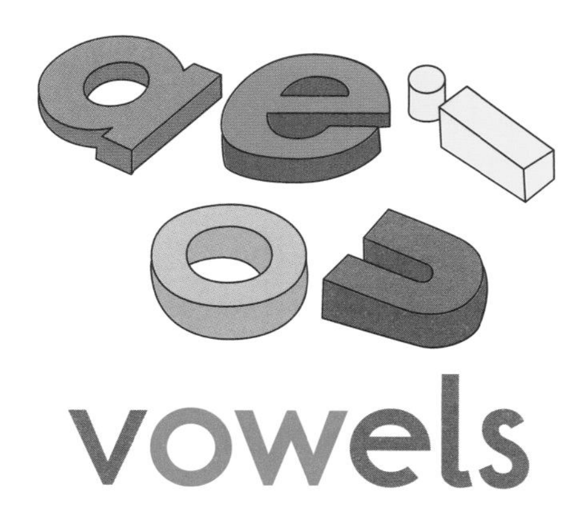

vowels

cow

town

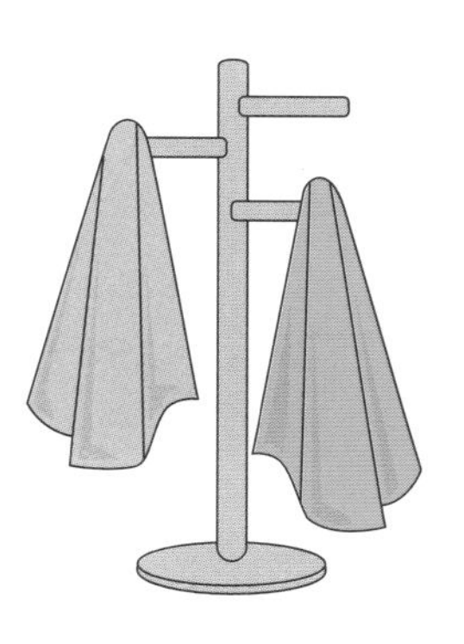

towels

shower

Phonics Online

Listen to the story about Oscar Orange and Walter Walrus. Sing along to the song, listen to the sound and play the games.

When you have finished this page, complete the ow activities in *Workbook 2*, pages 68-70.

Word Building

Build some **ow** words using *Phonics Online*, or the *Picture Code Cards*.

Code Card

Build it!

town, cow,
shower,
brown, now.

Let's read!

Read the words, then point to the correct picture.

The brown and black cows are in the town.

Listen to the song. If you can, join in with the chorus when you listen for the second time.

Story

Let's see what happens when Walter Walrus hides in Uppy's letter next to Oscar Orange in a word.

Walter Walrus's water tricks!

Watch out when Walter Walrus is about! Walter likes to splash water.

Now look what Walter has done. He's filled Uppy Umbrella's letter with salty water so he can splash Oscar with it.

As he splashes he slips and

bumps his chin again.

They both shout,

'Ou!'

Use your *Picture Code Cards* to review the sound.

Explore

Listen to the story about Walter hiding in Uppy's letter.

Oscar Orange & Walter in Uppy's letter

Listen again to the story. This time look for the things in the picture in which you can hear Oscar and Walter shouting, '**ou**!'

Keywords

Find these items in the picture. Listen out for Oscar and Walter shouting, '**ou**!' in them.

mountain

fountain

clouds

mouse

house

Phonics Online

Listen to the story about Oscar Orange and Walter in Uppy's letter.
Sing along to the song, listen to the sound and play the games.

Workbook

When you have finished this page, complete the **ou** activities in *Workbook 2*, pages 71-73.

Word Building

Build some **ou** words using *Phonics Online*, or the *Picture Code Cards*.

Build it!

loud, cloud,
round, sound.

Let's read!

Read the words.
Then point to the correct picture.

That house has a round window.

We like to make a loud sound.

Listen to the song. If you can, join in with the chorus when you listen for the second time.

Phonics Readers

Read the stories in *Phonics Readers 9*, featuring the phonic elements in this Unit.

Comprehension

Point to the correct answer.

1. What did Firefighter Fred add to the drawing?

○ a fawn ☐ a drink

2. What did Harry Hat Man add to the drawing?

○ a horse ☐ a hawk

3. Where does the mouse live?

○ in a shop ☐ in a round hole

4. What is the name of the cat in the story?

○ Miss Brown ☐ Miss Frown

5. What did the boys eat for lunch?

○ fresh crab ☐ fresh trout

Pair work

When you have read the stories, the teacher will read the questions. Work in pairs or small groups to read and point to the correct answers.

Stickers Complete the sticker activity in *Workbook 2*, page 74.

Listen Complete the exercises in *Workbook 2*, pages 75-77.

Talk time

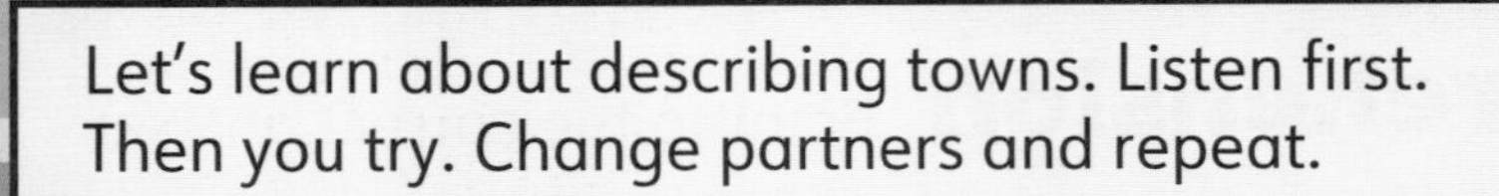

Let's learn about describing towns. Listen first.
Then you try. Change partners and repeat.

Post Office

Find the...
- Restaurant
- Bank
- Hospital
- Post Office
- Park
- Museum
- Hotel
- School

Where is the... ?
- It's next to the...
- It's opposite the...
- It's in front of the...
- It's behind the...

Can you count?
How many...
- cars?
- trucks?
- traffic lights?
- zebra crossings?

Pair work Work in pairs. First, find all the buildings in the picture. Then ask each other where they are. Finally, practise some counting!

Quick Dash

Now you know all of the spelling patterns for Level 2. Use your *Picture Code Cards* to quickly revise them.

Revise all the sounds and spelling patterns using the *Phonics Online* Cards Tool, or the *Picture Code Cards*. Go through them as quickly as you can.

Quick!

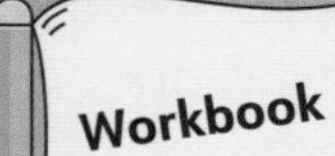

When you have completed a Quick Dash, there is a short test in *Workbook 2*, pages 78-79.

Read the stories in *Phonics Readers 10*, featuring the phonic elements in this Unit.

Comprehension

Point to the correct answer.

1. What did the girl do in her dream?

○ sat on a shark □ pulled a shark

2. Find the name of the person who swims with sharks.

○ Dad and Pip □ Dr E. Clark

3. What did Bouncy Ben bring to the garden?

○ peas □ beans

4. What did Munching Mike plant in the garden?

○ melons □ men

5. Who helped Golden Girl pick the crops?

○ her mum □ her gran

Pair work

When you have read the stories, the teacher will read the questions. Work in pairs or small groups to read and point to the correct answers.